Old Partick
Lewis Hutton

The compact site of Dowanhill Park was purchased by Glasgow Corporation in 1903, to preserve an open space among the tenements that were being erected in the district. Two sites were considered, the other one being on North Gardner Street, now occupied by Partickhill Bowling Club. The park was opened in August 1905 by Bailie McMillan convenor of the Parks Committee, followed by prayers and speeches to the assembled crowd. The invited guests then made their way to Partick Burgh Hall for wine and cake hosted by Provost William Kennedy. Behind the boys is the drinking fountain unveiled that day, which still stands in the centre of the park, a product of the Saracen Foundry in Possilpark. Dowanhill School on the right was built in 1896 on land acquired from the Dowanhill Estate Company by Govan Parish School Board. The school was, at the time, the most expensive constructed for the board and had accommodation for 1,579 pupils. In 2013 it became Notre Dame Primary School with a more modest 460 students.

Author's Note

The most obvious boundary for Partick is that of the police burgh established in 1852. This would make for a wide-ranging book that covers a large swathe of western Glasgow from the Kelvin through Partick and Partickhill, Broomhill, Thornhill, Whiteinch and up to Jordanhill Station. It's a big area. Instead I have drawn the line at the railway bridge over Dumbarton Road in the west and, Highburgh Road, not including Partickhill in the north, as the core of Partick. It covers the old village and the area surrounding it. The book includes the lands of Overnewton, on the east bank of the Kelvin which despite being in Glasgow were often thought of as Partick. To anyone looking for a book on the parts not covered I apologise, but hope you enjoy *Old Partick*.

© Lewis Hutton, 2024
First published in the United Kingdom, 2024,
by Stenlake Publishing Ltd.
54-58 Mill Square, Catrine, KA5 6RD
www.stenlake.co.uk
ISBN 978-1-84033-983-3

The publishers regret that they cannot supply copies of any pictures featured in this book.

Printed by
P2D Books, 1 Newlands Rd, Westoning, Bedford MK45 5LD

Further Reading

The following were the principal books and websites used by the author during his research. Except *Along Great Western Road* none are available from Stenlake Publishing; please contact your local bookshop, reference library or search for them on the internet.

Boyce, David, *Bridges of the Kelvin*, 1996
Clarkson, Tim, *Strathclyde and the Anglo-Saxons in the Viking Age*, 2014
Hume, John, *Industrial Archaeology of Glasgow*, 1974
Kinchin, Perilla and Juliet, *Glasgow's Great Exhibitions, 1888, 1901, 1911, 1938, 1988*, 1988
Napier, James, *Notes and Reminiscences Relating to Partick*, 1853.
Ness, James (1st Ed 1891), and others, *The Incorporation of Bakers of Glasgow*, 2001 (5th Edition).
Smart, Aileen, *Villages of Glasgow*, vol 1, 1988
Spalding, Bill, *Bygone Partick*, 1992
— *Bygone Partick 2*, 1992
Taylor, Charles, *Partick – Past and Present*, 1902
Urquart, Gordon, *Along Great Western Road*, 2000

Too many websites were consulted for them all to be listed. Of particular use were those of The British Newspaper Archive and National Library of Scotland. Glasgow Punter's blog deserves a mention for its piece on the history of Hyndland After School Club.

Tickets from the last days of the Underground before its 1970s modernisation. Before closure in May 1977 a fare stage system was operated and these cheap tickets from Merkland Street paid for a journey of a couple of stations, for more distant stations a 15p or even 20p ticket was needed. After it reopend in November 1979 a flat fare carried passengers wherever they wanted.

Introduction

Partick owes its existence to the River Clyde. Downstream from its confluence with the Kelvin the river split forming islands separated by shallow easily-forded channels. The Partick-Govan ford was one of the most important of these, less affected by tides than those closer to the sea. This was reflected by the growth of both settlements Govan become a centre of Christianity perhaps as early as the 5th century and Partick developed into a royal centre. They were part of the Kingdom of Alt Clut ruled from the citadel of Dumbarton Rock. In 870 the rock was sacked by Viking raiders, and the twin settlements of Partick and Govan became the seat of power in the reformed kingdom. Church and government were south of the river which ultimately lead to the formation of Govan Parish. Encompassing both banks of the Clyde and a pocket of land at Pointhouse its extent seems odd now but makes more sense in its ancient context. As part of Govan Parish, residents of Partick were expected to attend church in Govan. As a result there was no dedicated church in the village until 1824. Partick, with its royal connection, was the property of kings until it was gifted to the Archbishops of Glasgow in 1136.

A village grew up in the lee of the royal residence, on the banks of the River Kelvin. The river's fast-flowing water made it ideal for milling. This industry expanded considerably in the 12th century, when Glasgow outgrew the Molendinar Burn's ability to provide power for mills. In the 1820s there were six mills on the half-mile of river, from Clayslaps to the Slit Mill. By that time they had all been converted to flour mills providing for the nearby city. The Slit Mill, for example, owed its name to the fact it once slit sheets of iron to make nails before it was converted to flour milling in the 1780s.

While flour dominated Kelvin's mills, the Industrial Revolution diversified Partick's manufacturing. David Dale, George Macintosh, and Pierre Jacques Papillon built their dyeworks and bleachfield in Dalmarnock in 1785. Its success led to them developing several more sites, including one in Partick at Meadowside. The dyeworks burned a few years later and was abandoned for their Vale of Leven enterprise. The Lancefield Spinning Company established a power-loom in Castlebank Street. Shipbuilding came to Partick in 1844 when David Tod and John McGregor bought the old bleachfield at Meadowside for their new yard. One of the first ships built there was the *City of Glasgow* the first screw-powered steamer to cross the Atlantic. Their dry-dock, constructed in 1858, was considered so impressive that it became a tourist attraction.

Partick's industry caused its population to increase from 1,235 in 1820, to 5,043 in 1851. This allowed the village to take advantage of the Police of Towns (Scotland) Act, 1850, and become a Police Burgh. The Act and its previous iteration in 1833, in addition to the obvious control of law and order, provided the commissioners of the burgh oversight of water supplies and sewerage; cleansing; street maintenance, lighting, and paving; and public health. A meeting, held in November 1851, highlighted the need to remedy most of these issues, and the following year in June they formed Partick Police Burgh with twelve commissioners. From that number three were elected as magistrates, one of whom, David Tod, became the first Provost of Partick. One of their first acts was to improve drainage and sanitation.

The continual growth of Glasgow began to threaten Partick's existence as an independent polity and proposals were made to extend the city westward. The first of several attempts to annex Partick came in 1869 and was resisted. The Glasgow Municipal Extension Bill prompted discussion, in 1875, among the commissioners of Partick, Hillhead and Maryhill about combining their burghs into a larger entity. They had created a unified gas company in 1871, and considered building a hospital for the three burghs at Anniesland Cross. Maryhill wasn't keen on the political union and the plans died. Co-operation continued between Partick and Hillhead; together they tried to annex Dowanhill and Kelvinside in 1881. They were supported by the superiors of the districts but popular opinion was against the merger and it failed. The failure prompted Kelvinside to try to annex itself and Hillhead to Glasgow. Debate raged for several years and ended with Hillhead, Kelvinside and Maryhill being absorbed by the city in 1891. Partick stood alone, with continual pressure to become part of Glasgow and in 1912 it did.

Partick has been a suburb of Glasgow ever since, its history of milling perhaps influencing the site of the Meadowside Granary. The 1950s and 60s saw traditional heavy industries begin to move out of the city to larger sites or to close altogether. The cramped housing south of Dumbarton Road was swept away and its residents moved to Dalmuir and Drumchapel. Shipbuilding at Meadowside ended in 1935 and other industries were lost. Partick saw a long decline into the 1990s, and a millennium of milling ended in 2013. More recently, through the efforts of community groups and organisations like Partick Housing Association, it is looking brighter and busier. The new Riverside Museum has reclaimed the derelict land at Pointhouse, and a new bridge remakes an ancient river crossing to Govan.

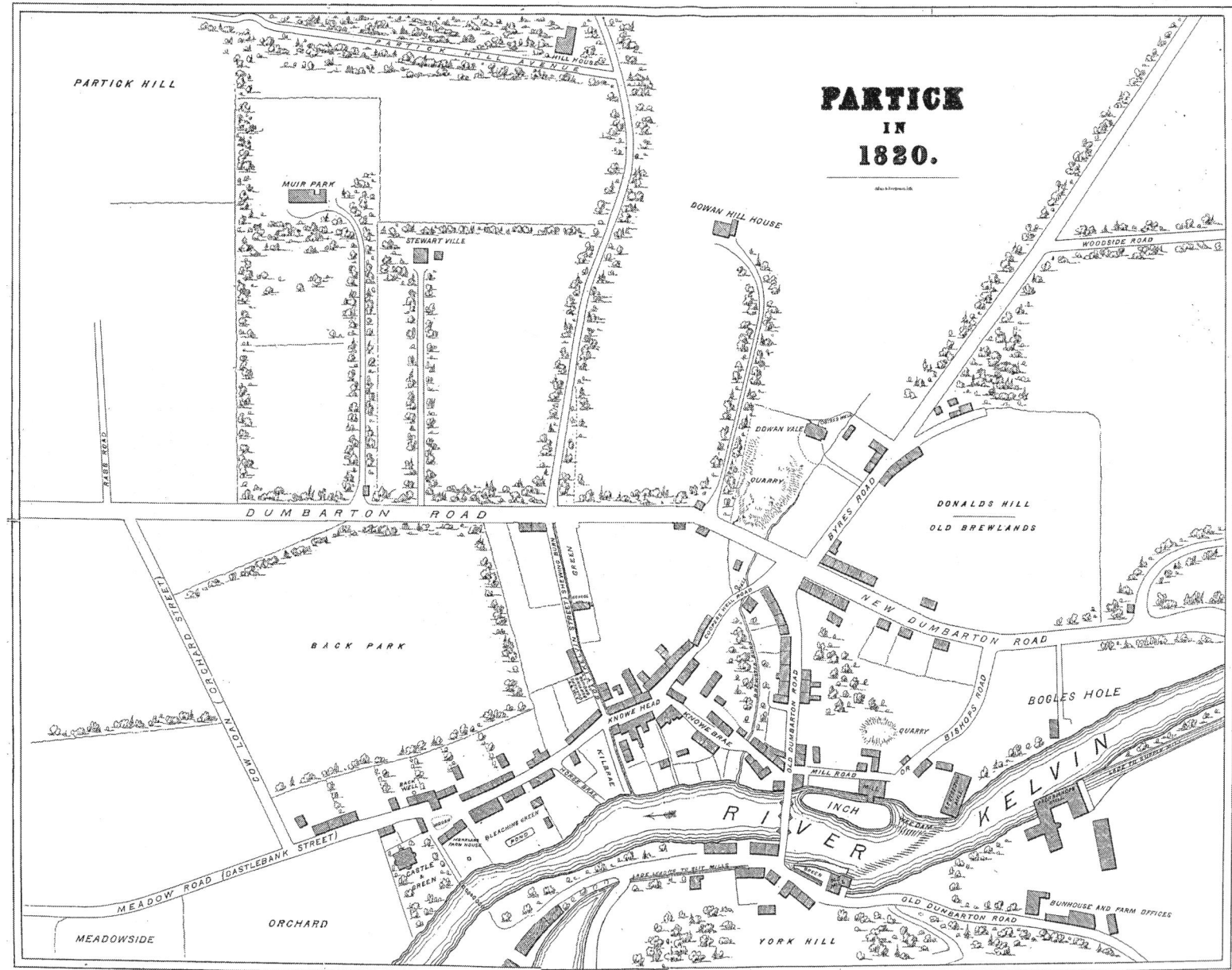

A remnant of old Partick, probably in Castlebank Street, with the tenements in Douglas Street [Purdon Street] behind. In the 1880s the western corner of Castlebank and Douglas Streets was redeveloped, and a new row of tenements constructed on the site of the old buildings. Castlebank Street continued east from the junction with Douglas Street. A famous inn and brewhouse stood at the north-west corner of the junction. Bonnie Prince Charlie met his officers there during their occupation of Glasgow, from 26th December 1745 to the 3rd January before continuing their retreat north.

The first mention of a Partick castle comes from one source, the hagiographer Jocelin of Furness who in his account of the life of St. Kentigern tells us that in the 6th Century King Rhydderch Hael of Alt Clut had a residence there. It was Rydderch's queen Languoreth, who lost the ring later recovered from a fish by Kentigern that forms one of the saint's four miracles, perhaps performed in Partick. By the 9th century the Kingdom of Alt Clut had become Strat Clut and had moved its capital to Govan, and King Arthgal's main residence was Partick Castle. The Strathclyde Kingdom became part of Scotland possibly around 1030, and the royal estate passed to the Crown of Scotland. King David I granted the lands and castle to the Bishops of Glasgow in 1136, who continued to use the castle until the Reformation in 1560. The site of this earlier castle is unknown, but it may have been reused when George Hutcheson built his Partick Castle in 1611. Some of the artefacts found in 2016 during an archaeological dig suggest that this is the case. By 1770 the small windows and tight staircase of Hutcheson's tower house were old fashioned, it was abandoned and quickly fell to the ruin seen in this engraving of the castle next to Merkland Farm. In the mid-19th century the castle was cleared and its foundations buried by a succession of industries.

Looking south towards the west side of old Partick Bridge, built in the late 16th century, at the lowest, narrowest, point on the Kelvin that a solid rock foundation could be obtained. Until 1800 it was the main crossing point for travellers heading west from Glasgow, along the Dumbarton road.

The building closest to us is the Lower Scotstoun Mill which was usually called the Wee Mill, to differentiate it from the larger Scotstoun Mill just upstream. The River Kelvin was split by an island at this point with the Wee Dam channelling water past the mill. The larger Scotstoun Mill complex eventually took over the Wee Mill and turned it into a machine shop.

The ducks foraging in the mill pond were the focus of the Partick Duck Club, formed in 1810, by a mix of Glasgow merchants, bankers, shopkeepers and professors. On Saturdays they would gather at the Bunhouse Inn which was just south of where the Kelvin Hall is now and enjoy roast duck with peas. The name and spirit of the club is continued today by the restaurant in Hyndland Street.

The Bishop's Mill stands on the east side of Old Partick Bridge, on the site of a medieval mill. The mill was part of lands confiscated from the Church during the Reformation. Utilising the drop created by the adjacent waterfall this was one of the first mills on the river, and had priority on water drawn from it. Despite this advantage, the height of the mill dam across the top of the waterfall was controlled through an agreement with the Incorporation of Bakers of Glasgow who owned the upstream Bunhouse Mill. If the dam was too high the mill pond flooded the bottom of the Incorporation mill's wheels, and stopped them turning. The grain drying kiln of the Bishop's Mill caught fire in November 1836. Hopes of saving the building rested with the Anderston fire engines and a rider was dispatched to fetch them. Unfortunately they demanded a guarantee of expenses to save the building and so the rider had to return to Partick to secure the assurance of payment before the engines were dispatched. The delay, unsurprisingly, meant that when they arrived the fire was out of control and the building burned to the ground. Fortunately no-one was hurt and most of the stored grain was saved. The mill, rebuilt in 1839, still stands and was converted to flats in 1987.

Old Partick Bridge survived until 1895 when it was demolished during construction of the Lanarkshire and Dumbarton Railway.

St. Peter's Church on Bridge Street [Partick Bridge Street] was the first Roman Catholic church in Partick, opening in 1858. The church closed in 1903 when its replacement on Hyndland Street opened, but because of Partick's increasing population it reopened in 1923, serving as an extension to the main church and known as Bridge Street Chapel. On the right of this picture is the corner of St. Peter's School which opened in 1864. It closed in 1924 after its pupils were moved to Stewartville Street School.

The interior of St. Peter's Church looking to the sanctuary. During the Second World War Polish soldiers based at Yorkhill and the wider Polish community in exile began worshipping at the church. In response the Catholic Church created a new parish for Yorkhill called St Simon's in 1945 – Simon was St. Peter's original name until Biblical translations transformed it into Peter, changing the man Jesus called a rock to the Latin *Petra* and then Peter. The church was renovated in 1956 and more extensively in 2008 supported by Historic Scotland. The restoration was rendered futile in 2021, when an arson attack left only the walls standing. With the cost of restoration projected to be several million the site was sold to Partick Housing Association to build flats.

Partick Subscription School in Kelvin Street [Keith Street] with Partick Rubber Works behind it. The school was established as a trust on 23rd June 1790 to educate the children, boys and girls, of the village in 'English language, writing and arithmetic'. It built on the legacy of a similar school established 40 years prior that had fallen into disrepair. In spite of the trustees' best efforts to create an organisation that could withstand their passing, the Subscription School's trust broke down, hastened by the Disruption of the Scottish Church in 1843. This coincided with the growth of church schools which superseded the old institution. By the time of this photograph in the 1880s it wes occupied by joiner John Buchanan whose cart can be seen in the playground behind the former school.

Keith Street at its junction with Dumbarton Road around the turn of the 20th century. Originally this was Kelvin Street but was renamed along with many others in the 1920s, to avoid duplication of street names across Glasgow. The street was also known as The Goat, after the Scots word for ditch, which flowed along the east side. Both the Goat Burn and the Brewlands Burn (which rose near Dowan Vale House in Byres and flowed to the Kelvin near the old bridge), were culverted in the early 19th century. The Quaker Burial Ground on Kelvin Street (now off Keith Court) was established in 1711 by the Purdon family. It provided a resting place for Margaret Purdon, a Quaker, who had married into the family. Other Christian denominations forbade Quaker burials in their cemeteries so the family set aside some of their land which extended west from Kelvin Street for the purpose. It was last used in 1857.

The western extremity of the area covered by this book where the railway bridge crosses over Dumbarton Road, looking east toward the city. Partick's much missed Woolworth shop sits on the other side. The shop, Glasgow's tenth, opened September 1956 – not long before this photograph was taken – it closed in 2009 with the collapse of the chain. *The King and I* played at the Rosevale Cinema Dumbarton Road, in January 1957. The entrance to Partick Hill Station is on the left. The North British Railway constructed the Stobcross Railway connecting Maryhill to Stobcross Quay in 1874, and in 1882 opened Partick Station on the north side of Dumbarton Road; it became Partick Hill in 1953. The station closed in 1979 when the new Partick Station was opened on Merkland Street.

Dumbarton Road at its junction with Peel Street named for Prime Minister Robert Peel, mainly for his championing the repeal of the Corn Laws, which earned him considerable respect. In 1870 the Glasgow Street Tramways Act was passed, and by November 1875 the Glasgow Tramway and Omnibus Company's line from Union Street had reached a few yards beyond the railway bridge on Dumbarton Road. Drivers frequently refused to stop at Peel Street and carried on to the terminus causing friction between residents and the tramway company, and at least a couple of minor accidents as passengers tried and misjudged jumping from a moving tram. The inconvenience was brief as the tram line soon extended further west to Whiteinch with Peel Street becoming another stop along the way. The tramway was taken over by Glasgow Corporation Tramways in 1894, soon after they began to modernise the network replacing the horse-drawn trams with electric ones like No. 122 heading for Scotstoun.

Looking north into Peel Street from Dumbarton Road, then as now the corner shop is occupied by a baker. On the opposite corner is St. Mary's Partick Parish Church which was opened by the Church of Scotland in August 1863. The first sermon was delivered by the Rev. Dr Leishman of Govan Parish, who drew attention to the fact that this was the seventh church erected in Partick during his ministry. The first had been in 1843 when there were 3,000 people living in the burgh and now there were 17,000. A century later, with declining church attendance, it merged with Dowanvale and Partick High churches to become Hamilton Crescent Parish Church. Further mergers occurred in 1978 when the congregation joined Partick South Church. The building of St. Mary's Church was surplus to requirements and was demolished in 1987, to be replaced by flats.

The West of Scotland Cricket Ground in Hamilton Crescent [Fortrose Street since 1931] has a long sporting history. Before the eponymous club existed the Clutha Cricket Club played matches on its grass. Some of the Clutha members had the grand plan to form a MCC for Scotland and established the West of Scotland club in 1862 adopting the ground as their home turf. In 1872, the first international football match was held there between Scotland and England drawing a crowd of 4,000. Six years later 8,000 spectators were present for a cricket match between the West of Scotland Club and Australia, which ended in a sporting draw. The ground continues to be used for both domestic and international cricket. The bowling greens of Partick Bowling and Peel Street Bowling Clubs which moved in 1870 to become Annfield Bowling Club, were established on the surrounding ring of streets. Partick Curling Club's pond was next to the green on Peel Street. They came to the street in 1856 from the pond that used to be opposite the Curlers Tavern in Byres Road, and moved again in 1893 to Victoria Park.

Facing page: Partick Academy was established in 1851 to educate the growing middle and upper classes of the burgh. Its first school was in Church Street off Byres Road, which it sold to Govan Parish School Board in 1877. In preparation for the sale this new school was built at 75 Peel Street for £8,000, and opened 30th August 1878. The school board entered negotiations with the academy in 1883 to purchase the Peel Street building but quickly decided that it was too small and the sale price too high so resolved to build their own. Their Hamilton Crescent School, now Hyndland Primary, opened in 1887. The competition was too much for the academy which closed the same year. The building lay empty for a few years before it became the Academy Rooms used for dances, functions and meetings. Whether it was the Boilermaker's Society planning a shipyard strike, Women's Freedom League lectures, or Committee meetings for Partick Wanderers the rooms hosted them all. In October 1917 the building was purchased by the YMCA, whose activities at their Western Institute continued until the mid-1960s, after which the building began to decay. It was demolished in the early 1970s.

Partick Free High Church stood on the corner of Peel Street and Fortrose Street. Following the Disruption of 1843 the Free Church split from the Church of Scotland and there followed a rush to build churches for the new denomination, including this one designed by John Honeyman, built in 1869. Reunification of the denominations saw this church become part of the Church of Scotland in 1929 as Partick High Church. The congregation merged with St. Mary's Partick in 1963 leaving the building empty. It became the evangelical City Temple Church, though by the late 1970s it was empty and suffered a mysterious fire in 1980, after which it was demolished and flats built on the site.

Hamilton Crescent School was opened in May 1887 as a secondary with space for 1,000 pupils. It is one of the few buildings still standing today in this c.1905 photograph, the others being the terrace on the left and the villa below it. When Hyndland School opened on Clarence Drive in 1912, it became Hamilton Crescent Supplementary School. Despite many of the staff and pupils moving to the new school the one on Hamilton Crescent continued to grow; the mansion that stood immediately to its north became an annexe in 1913. Its grounds provided space for a gymnasium to be built, which in 1932 was joined by a drill hall. The latter served for many years as the school's dining hall and now houses the After School Club. Collingwood Villa, on the corner of Hamilton Crescent, was purchased in 1934. The intention was to demolish it and build a new extension but it instead became another annexe. The school was designated a junior secondary in 1940 and its senior pupils left to study at Hyndland Senior Secondary which shared its site with Hyndland Primary. The descision to consolidate secondary teaching on Clarence Drive was made in 1972, and Hyndland Primary moved to Partick! The Collingwood Villa was demolished in 1975. Its grounds became the upper playground of the new primary school. In the early 2000s, the 1913 annexe was demolished and a new extension built to the school connecting the main building to the gymnasium.

One of the few surviving parts of old Partick south of Dumbarton Road are the former burgh offices on the corner of Anderson and Gullane Streets. When Partick became a police burgh in 1852 these were built to house its newly-established police force and courts. Meetings of the Burgh Commissioners took place in a number of halls across Partick, frequently the Princess's Halls in Merkland Street. It wasn't until November 1869 that the commissioners began to seriously discuss the necessity of a burgh hall. The West of Scotland Cricket club were asked and agreed that a portion of their ground could be acquired for the purpose. A site on the western side of Hyndland Street, then part of the estate of Stewartville House, was also investigated. Maxwell Street [Burgh Hall Street] was the preferred location and in April 1870 intimation was given that ground had been acquired there. On the 1st October 1872 the opening ceremony, for the French Renaissance style building designed by William Leiper, was held. The tenements on Maxwell Street were acquired in 1902 and converted to offices. In 1912 Partick was annexed by Glasgow and ended the hall's use as a council chamber, but it continues to serve as a venue for meetings, events and weddings.

Looking north along Merkland Street to Dumbarton Road and the entrance to Peel Street. The street once ran south from this point to Castlebank Street but that was cleared in the 1960s. For several years the site lay empty before plans were approved for the Merkland Street Shopping Centre in 1975, with space for a supermarket and other small shops. The original supermarket was owned by Presto which by way of Safeway has become Morrisons, slowly incorporating the premises of the smaller shops in the centre. Merkland Street was the location of one of Partick's Subway stations distinguished as the only one to have been closed. The ghost station is about 25 metres down the line in the direction of Govan from its replacement. Partick Station, a new interchange opened December 1979, linking newly-built railway and Subway stations. As part of that plan bus stances were built on Merkland Street where the buildings on the near right of this photograph stand.

No photograph of Gardner Street ever shows it off properly, and it never looks as steep as it does in the imagination of anyone who has trudged their way to the top. Hyndland Primary pupils from Hyndland and Dowanhill, including myself, walked to and from the school over its lofty summit. Memorably one winter a pipe burst causing a sheet of ice near the junction with Partickhill Road. We were saved from a long detour via Caird Drive by a group of young men, who with ropes and climbing equipment assisted pupils on their traverse up the new Partick glacier. Before the street was built the land was the grounds of Muirpark mansion, which stood roughly where White Street crosses. In 1881 the house and gardens were rented by John Mcleod, who opened a waxworks exhibit and menagerie. The lower part of the grounds, on the flat near Dumbarton Road, were leased to Partick Thistle where they played until 1885. That year John Gardner bought the estate, evicted its lessees and began fueing the land on either side of a road running straight through the former grounds and mansion of Muirpark, which he named Gardner Street after himself.

Stewartville School dominates the view in this photograph of Stewartville Street. The school was opened in November 1891 by Govan Parish School Board in response to Partick's growing population, which had increased by about 10,000 in ten years to 36,538 people. The new school was well-equipped, had a 50 feet long swimming pool in the basement, and places for 1,450 pupils. After the First World War it became an annexe to St. Peter's School and after the school in Bridge Street closed in 1924 became the St. Peter's (boys) School. It closed in 1981 and has since been converted to flats. The street, in common with Gardner Street to its west, was formed on the estate of a mansion, Stewartville House, which stood near the church behind the school. Billy Connolly both lived in the street and attended the school as a pupil, and credited his experiences there for forming his desire to make people laugh.

Dumbarton Road photographed looking east from the foot of Stewartville Street. Dominating the scene on the right of the picture is Newton Place Church. Prior to 1823 Partick members of the Relief Church – which split from the Church of Scotland in 1761 – worshipped in Anderston. After briefly worshipping in an old power-loom factory on Castlebank Street, they built Newton Place Relief Church on Dumbarton Road in 1824. That church was demolished to make way for the one in the photograph which opened 8th January 1865 as Partick West United Presbyterian Church – the Relief and United Succession churches joined to become the United Presbyterians in 1847. The 20th century saw the decline of congregation numbers and amalgamation of churches, which were, in Partick, consolidated here becoming Partick South Church in 1978. The Victorian building was demolished in 1988 and a modern church constructed in its place. It is survived by its hall tucked away in a corner of the church grounds. The buildings in front of the church were demolished in the 1920s to make way for new tenements and Partick Library which opened in 1925.

Hyndland Street looking north from its junction with Dumbarton Road. Originally known as Coarse Loan it ran along the northern part of Partick Green which also extended south from here along the side of Kelvin Street [Keith Street]. When the Glasgow to Yoker Turnpike, or Dumbarton Road, was laid out in the late-18th century it cut through the green. The northern portion was absorbed into the grounds of Dowanhill House. The southern portion, known as the School Green, was vigorously defended as an open space, used for public announcements and open air sermons until the 1860s when it was fued and built on. In the distance is the spire of Dowanhill United Presbyterian Church, designed by William Leiper, his first solo commission, and opened in 1866. Scottish artist, Daniel Cottier, worked with Leiper designing the stained glass and furniture. After the congregation left, the Four Acres Charitable Trust was formed to restore the church, turning it into a bar and arts centre, including the Cottiers Theatre.

Hyndland Street looking south from its junction with White Street. On the left is St. Peter's Church and Presbytery opened in 1903 after the Roman Catholic congregation outgrew its church on Partick Bridge Street. Seeing an opportunity Grant's Newsagents opened a new branch on the opposite corner of White Street, with an 'Excellent supply of Irish and Catholic newspapers', and that 'rosaries and other pious objects are available in great variety at wholesale prices'. The tenements on the left hand side of the street were demolished in the late 1960s creating a piece of waste ground, which was empty for several years before it was redeveloped as Mansfield Park returning the land to common use. The open space was much appreciated, though underused, and sparse, with a blaes football pitch taking up most of it, which served as a venue for the Partick Farmer's Market. In 2008 the park was redesigned, removing the pitch, and landscaping with trees and a paved area next to Dumbarton Road for the market.

Looking west along White Street from Hyndland Street, to its junctions with Stewartville and Gardner Streets, following the line of the northern boundary of the Stewartville House grounds. The street was named for the second Provost of Partick John White, who owned Scotstoun Mill on the River Kelvin. The street used to end at this junction and the continuation of the line to Byres Road was called Wood Street. It was renamed along with many other streets in Partick in 1931 to avoid duplication of Glasgow street names. There were two other Wood Streets in the city, the one off Alexandra Parade was chosen to retain its name with the Partick and Port Dundas ones forced to change.

In 1895 St. Peter's acquired the land between Hyndland and Dowanhill Streets, where they intended to build their new church and a school. The school on Dowanhill Street opened in 1899 catering for girls and infants – boys were taught at the school on Bridge Street and later Stewartville Street School. It closed in 2013 and merged with Notre Dame Primary at the former Dowanhill Primary School. The disused building was purchased by Partick Housing Association who demolished it in 2017 and built 60 flats on the site. Just off the right of the photograph was the site of Dowanhill House which was sold for feuing in 1900, its once extensive estate had by that time been reduced to a plot bounded by tenements to the west and Dowanhill, Lawrence and White Streets on its other sides.

Byres Road is named after the hamlet of Byres which sat a little to the north of Partick village. roughly where Torness Street is. Named for the byres owned by the Bishop's of Glasgow which had been located there. From there the old road, often called the Roman road headed north west towards Hyndland Road, and formed part of the drove route for cattle from the Highlands. By the 18th century the road was in a state of disrepair its ancient origins had been long forgotten. It was described as being laid of large flat bottomed stones with smaller stones providing infill, prompting association with the Romans. The owner of Dowanhill House made several attempts and was ultimately successful in closing the right-of-way in the late 18th century, forcing the old road north and leading to the formation of the modern Byres Road, which is seen in this photograph looking north from the junction with Havelock Street.

At the foot of Byres Road where it meets Dumbarton Road is Partick Cross, joined from the south (left) by Well Street [Cooperswell Street] and Bridge Street. The cross began to develop in the 18th century with the formation of the Glasgow and Yoker Turnpike. Its present configuration dates to 1800 when the turnpike's first Dumbarton Road Bridge was built over the River Kelvin, giving the road a more direct route to the west and avoiding the narrow Partick Bridge. Partick Mansions on the right-hand side with Hepworth's shop occupy the site of the first church in Partick which opened in 1823, not long before the church in Newton Place. The congregation were of the United Secession Church and became Partick East United Presbyterian Church when the Relief and Secession Churches united in 1847. Hepworth was a man's clothing shop established 1884 in Huddersfield with branches across Britain, and was the largest clothing retailer in the country. By the 1980s they had branched into women's clothing but sales were declining, so the women's clothing shops were rebranded as Next. The rebranding was phenomenally successful and in 1985 their men's shops were rebranded too, ending the Hepworth name on the high street.

The 18th century saw two splits in the Church of Scotland, the first in 1733 leading to a number of further divisions and amalgamations until the formation of the United Secession Church in 1820. The second of the splits in 1761 led to the formation of the Relief Church. In 1824 both had established their own places of worship in Partick. Those who remained with the Church of Scotland were still obliged to worship in Govan. Anxious for a more convenient place of worship, and one that avoided the possibility of accidental baptism in the Clyde a petition was made to the Session of Govan for their own church. The request was granted and a site was gifted by Archibald Bogle of Gilmorehill, on the western side of what would become Church Street. The Partick Old Parish Church opened in March 1834, and was completely rebuilt in 1879. The photograph of the interior was taken in 1934 for the centenary. The congregation merged with Partick Trinity Church in 1990, after which Old Parish Church became a furniture warehouse. At that time the stained glass was removed and preserved, preventing its destruction in the fire which reduced the church to a ruin in 2002. New flats and commercial premises now occupy its site.

Dumbarton Road looking west from near the bridge over the River Kelvin. The Anderson College building of Glasgow University is just off the right of the photograph. This view has been utterly changed since this photograph was taken c.1900, and all the buildings in it have been replaced. At that time only the central part of the road was well maintained as a consequence of the tramway company's founding act which stipulated the area surrounding the tracks was laid in hard-stone setts. On either side of the cobbled section was metalled road, but in the words of a correspondent to the *North British Daily Mail* in 1881 it was 'always in a broken-up dirty-looking state, not to mention the risk of splashed boots or even dislocated ankle in getting on or off a car [tram]'. Further disquiet was raised over the noise of traction engines on the road. These were allowed by the turnpike trust to travel along the road at any hour because, unlike Glasgow, Partick lacked the bylaws to prevent them.

The second Dumbarton Road bridge looking south from the first. The older bridge, which is now used as a footpath, was very different when it was built in 1800. Subsequent rebuilding raised the level of its deck and widened it, these modifications and the increasing amount of traffic over it caused the bridge to settle throwing parts of it out of plumb, making it unsafe. The new wider bridge in the photograph was built in 1875 by the Glasgow and Yoker Turnpike Trust – which was formed in 1845 to properly maintain and repair the road. The bridge was built on a new alignment, straightening the awkward bend the old one forced on Dumbarton Road. Behind the tram is the chimney and building of Partick Sewage Pumping Station. It was built by Glasgow Corporation to take the flow from two local sewers and lift it to a higher one that takes it west to Dalmuir sewage treatment plant. Originally the pumps were steam powered but in the 1960s they were replaced by electric ones, rendering the chimney redundant, and it was removed in the 1970s. On the left of the photograph the advert for the Co-op's Lofty Peak flour adorns the Regent Mill, while Spillers name is on the adjacent Scotstoun Mill.

When Partick became a police burgh in 1852 its eastern boundary was fixed at the River Kelvin, running from the river mouth to the Old Dumbarton Bridge before crossing Gilmourhill and reaching Byres Road. Public perception might have seen the buildings and settlements at Bunhouse, Yorkhill, Pointhouse, Kelvinhaugh, Overnewton and Clayslaps as part of Partick's hinterland, but these places were part of Glasgow, separated from the advancing edge of urban development at Anderston and Finnieston by the fields of Stobcross. The same year Partick gained its burgh status Glasgow bought land for its grand West End Park from the Kelvingrove and Woodlands estates. It quickly became a popular retreat for Glaswegians and Partickonians. Contained within the park was Kelvingrove House. Several proposals were made for its use, such as a park keepers [very grand] residence; a shelter, with galleries, for visitors to the park when it rained. In the late 1860s the plans coalesced around using it as a museum which opened in 1872. The land at Clayslaps was purchased, in 1870, adding to the area of the park. This brought the park to Dumbarton Road and provided an area which the Glasgow Agricultural Society used as a showground in the mid-1880s. The new land was also perfect as the site for the Glasgow International Exhibition of 1888. Announced in November 1886, and undoubtedly encouraged by Edinburgh's exhibition that year, Glasgow's town council voted unanimously to hold an exhibition on West End Park two years hence. The exhibition opened on 8th May 1888. Its main building, housing most of the exhibits, faced Dumbarton Road with towers and minarets borrowing elements from Moorish, Byzantine and Indian architecture in utter contrast to the tenements nearby, earning it the nickname of Baghdad by Kelvinside. The purpose of the exhibition was to show off Glasgow's contributions to art, industry and science. It was also hoped that there would be a healthy profit to contribute towards a new art gallery and museum, since it had been obvious from its opening that Kelvingrove House was too small and cramped for that purpose. One of the most popular exhibits at the exhibition was a recreation of the Bishop's Palace (left), part of the demolished Glasgow Castle, which was near the Cathedral. Built of wood, canvas and plaster and painted realistically, it housed archaeology and artefacts of Scottish History.

The 1888 exhibition was a huge success, and raised a profit of £41,700. With public subscription and other gifts there was enough money to construct the new Kelvingrove Museum and Art Gallery. Its foundation stone was laid in 1897, and plans were made to hold an exhibition in 1901 to celebrate its opening. As in 1888 a temporary building on Sandyford Street was constructed as the main exhibition hall, inspired once more by oriental designs. From there the grand avenue, a covered walkway and exhibition space connected it to the new gallery. The avenue continued across Dumbarton Road (it became Argyle Street after 1905) by a covered bridge to the machinery hall. Behind the main range the rest of the exhibition spread across the park, including several restaurants, the international pavilions of France, Japan, Russia, Canada and Ireland and the concert hall. The Kelvin had been cleaned and its water level raised for the 1888 exhibition and was once again used for boat trips, with gondoliers and electric launches plying its waters.

Left: The gloriously ornate entrance building of the Glasgow International Exhibition 1901, photographed from Radnor Street.

Below: The main gallery of Kelvingrove Museum during the 1901 exhibition. The pipe organ was in the exhibition's concert hall. It was purchased and moved to the gallery when the exhibition closed.

Free band music was provided and could be heard throughout the afternoon and evening, and if the boat trips on the Kelvin were too sedate there were more exciting entertainments. The Switchback Railway was on the west bank of the river which for 3d. would hurl its passengers back and forth. Circling around the Russian Pavilions was a miniature railway built in the USA. There was a shooting jungle and a rifle range for those with a sharp eye. And for the really daring there was the Canadian Water Chute, an enormous slide that plunged its flat bottomed boats into the Kelvin where they would skip to a rest on its surface. It was expensive at 6d. but described as a 'must' – admission to the entire exhibition was a shilling, just twice the chute's cost. The 1901 Exhibition was another success, and provided a good profit which was set against restoring the park, and providing an Art Purchase Fund for the new galleries.

The last of the three exhibitions to be held in Kelvingrove Park was in 1911, the Scottish Exhibition of National History, Art and Industry. The exhibition was intended to fund an endowment of a chair of Scottish History and Literature at Glasgow University. Smaller than in 1901 and occupying only the part of the park east of Kelvin Way, the exhibition's focus was on Scottish history. The ornate oriental style of its predecessors was replaced with a Scottish one. The Palace of History, its exterior inspired by Falkland Palace contained artefacts from Scotland's history. Across the Kelvin from it was the Auld Toon a faux-recreation of an old Scottish townscape. A mock tower house covered up the nearby Saracen Fountain. Its town hall was a facsimile of Dunbar's while most of the other buildings were modelled on Glasgow's few remaining ancient ones – many of which have since been lost. It was finished with an Olde Toffee Shoppe, Auld Tartan Shop and an Aitmeal Farl Shoppie (a baker) amongst other pleasures. Again the exhibition was a success, funding the university chair, with enough left over to help restore the park.

On the other side of Argyle Street from Kelvingrove were the Bunhouse Grounds owned by the Incorporation of Bakers. The open ground was used for football matches and was the site of the Machinery Hall during the 1901 Exhibition. In 1917 the grounds were chosen as the site for the second British Industries Fair held in the city, hosted in the purpose-built Kelvin Hall. The fair opened on 19th August 1918 and closed a month later. The hall was immediately requisitioned by the military to serve as a store. Released in 1919, in time for Glasgow's third British Industries Fair, the Kelvin Hall became an established venue in the city for exhibitions, flower shows and circuses; including the annual Housing and Health Exhibition photographed above. Then on the evening of 7th July 1925 a fire started which took hold of the entire wooden-building in minutes. Flames and sparks set fire to about 100 flats across the road in Blantyre Street. Embers also landed on the roof of Kelvingrove Museum where three, small and quickly contained, fires broke out. Six more serious fires became established on the roofs of buildings to the east of the main blaze; including the Kelvingrove Church, in Kelvingrove Street, which was left as a shell and later demolished, its site still an open space. Exhibitions were cancelled and on 10th July the city resolved to build a new Kelvin Hall. The new hall built of steel and stone rather than wood opened in 1927.

In 1909 Glasgow Corporation leased a portion of the Bunhouse Grounds to build the West End Roller Rink, opening in June that year, with a main rink and a smaller beginners one. Skating lasted only a few years. By 1915 it had stopped and the building was used for indoor bowling. After the Kelvin Hall opened it was used as an annexe which can be seen on the right of the photograph opposite. It survived the fire but was demolished to make way for the new hall.

St. Enoch's Church stood at the junction of Dumbarton Road and Old Dumbarton Road. It was an offshoot of St. Enoch Church in St. Enoch Square and split from its parent church during the Disruption of 1843. A temporary church in Waterloo Street served the congregation before they built this church in 1873 on its triangular site They were joined on Old Dumbarton Road by the congregation of Kelvinhaugh Church in 1935. The church was destroyed by a bomb in 1941. The ruin stood until the late 1960s when it was demolished and became the Kelvin Service Station, part of James Retson's business, of car hire and second-hand vehicles. It was too small a site to properly support those activities so concentrated on petrol sales which ended in 2013. The site was redeveloped as student accommodation with a Tesco Express at street level.

At the southern end of the Bunhouse Grounds was the site of the Regent's Mill. It stood on the site of the ancient Bunhouse Mill, itself a replacement for the Archbishop's Mill. After a fire destroyed the mill in 1886 the incorporation feued the land to John Ure. He had the mill in the photograph constructed, with warehouses along the road and the mill proper beside the river (right). In 1903 it was sold to the Scottish Co-operative and Wholesale Society. In 1966 the SCWS stopped milling at the site, and asked the incorporation – who were still the superior – if they could change the mills use to a hotel. The incorporation sold their rights in 1971 and shortly after the mill was in possession of Glasgow District Council who demolished it in 1978. The site is under the car park of the Kelvin Hall.

The castellated tower of Scotstoun Mill is visible on the right-hand edge of the photograph on the facing page. The earliest record of a mill here is from 1587 when a waulk mill was constructed for fulling woollen cloth, to make it more waterproof and insulating – like duffel cloth. William Wilkinshaw of Scotstoun was granted the mill in 1711 and at some point turned it into a corn mill changing its name to Scotstoun Mill. The White family took possession of the mill in 1834. Both John White – after whom White Street is named – and his son, also John, were Provosts of Partick. The mill was badly damaged in a fire in February 1909, which gave the opportunity to completely reconstruct and modernise the mill, seen in the photograph from 1910. The mill was bought by Spillers in 1933 and sold to Rank Hovis McDougall in 1978. The mill continued in operation until 2013 when it was closed, demolished and turned into student accommodation.

The Caledonian Railway built the Lanarkshire and Dunbartonshire Railway in 1896, from central Glasgow to Dumbarton. Its construction necessitated the demolition of the Old Partick Bridge and reclaiming a strip of land from the river to provide the site of Partick Central Station, which is seen looking east in this photograph. A new bridge was built to replace the old one which carries Benalder Street over the railway and river and provided a place for the station buildings. The Regent and Scotstoun Mills each had sidings from the railway, and a train of a few wagons is on the left of the latter's photograph. The line duplicated the older North British Railway line with its station at Partick Hill, and Dr Beeching's axe fell on the Caledonian line. It closed to passengers in 1964, though remained open for freight until 1978. The southern part of the site became a scrapyard, the northern part with the station building became wasteground. This was bought by Tesco, who upset the local community by demolishing the old station building without permission in 2007. Their proposed supermarket was blocked by local action and they sold the site. Soon afterwards student accommodation was built north of Benalder Street followed by more on the southern side in 2014.

Yorkhill House on the summit of Yorkhill. The hill's prominent location overlooking the confluence of the Kelvin and Clyde, and their fords, gave it a strategic position. Earthworks found on the hill in 1868 along with some of the few Roman artefacts found in Glasgow, suggested that they may have had a fort there. It is more likely that it was a local chief who traded with the Romans had his stronghold on the hill. In 1805 the estate was purchased from the lands of Overnewton by Robert Fulton Alexander who named his new estate and mansion Yorkhill. In 1914 the estate was sold to become the Royal Hospital for Sick Children, replacing the organisation's earlier hospital on Garnethill. The Queen Mother's Maternity Hospital was added to the site in 1964. Maternity and Children's services were concentrated at the new Queen Elizabeth University Hospital between 2010 and 2015. This left the Yorkhill hospital free to become West Glasgow Ambulatory Care Hospital housing the minor injury unit and outpatient services from the former Western Infirmary.

Before he bought the Yorkhill Estate Robert Fulton Alexander briefly lived here, Thornbank House. It was built around 1775, as the country retreat of a Glasgow banker. It sat behind the corner now made by the houses on Ferry Road and Centurion Way. The warehouses on Yorkhill Wharf and the chimney of Kelvinhaugh Cotton Factory are in the background on the right. The lowest mill on the Kelvin, the Slit Mill, was nearby. After the Bunhouse Grounds were covered by the Kelvin Hall the remainder of the Yorkhill Estate, south of the hospital, became the site of a football pitch known as Yorkhill Park. There junior teams such as Haugh Rovers, Partick Glencairn and Partick Avondale played their rivals. There was a pavilion at the Gilbert Street end of the pitch. The southern car park of the hospital now covers the playing field, while the staff parking area sits on the tennis courts. After the playing fields were lost, about the mid-1960s, the park became wasteground. This has since been reclaimed through community action and is now once again Yorkhill Park.

A blue train about to cross the bridge over the River Kelvin about 1962. To the right of the train is South Orchard Street which was later known as Otter Lane and the corner tenement beyond it stood on Muirhead and Anderson Streets, which is roughly where Beith Street crosses the latter now. From this bridge the railway line continues west to Partick Station and east to central Glasgow. The line was built by the North British Railway to connect Maryhill with Stobcross Quay. Intended as a goods line it didn't have any passenger stations and terminated at the harbour. When Partick Station opened in 1882 the line was still a dead end and trains had to travel via Maryhill to reach Glasgow. This would soon change with the completion of the City and District Railway in 1886. The new railway line connected Glasgow's High Street to Stobcross through the Queen Street Low Level Tunnel. The new shorter route through the tunnels was hugely popular, though the smoke and steam in their confines was frequently complained about. Perhaps unsurprisingly this was one of the first railways to be electrified in Scotland, the new clean service began in November 1960.

In 1962 the clearance of Castlebank Street was already under way. Undisturbed for now, is Archibald Jackson's public house at No. 82-84, the wall to its left guarding the Caledonian Railway's tunnel underneath the street.

A little to its west Otter Lane (*top right*) ran along the line of the former South Orchard Street to an underpass below the railway bridge. The existence of the lane has been erased, and student accommodation has been constructed over it.

Beyond the underpass an iron footbridge (*lower right*), on the south side of the railway bridge, was built to replace the old right of way provided by the stepping stones near Partick Castle. This was once the route of parishioners on their way to the ferry and church in Govan, later used by workers at A&J Inglis Pointhouse Shipyard. After the yard closed the bridge was removed *c.*1964. The bridge was also the vantage point of the photograph on the previous page, its high incurving sides more scalable than they look.

Taken from the high vantage point of the old footbridge A&J Inglis Yard at Pointhouse c.1962. The shipyard at Pointhouse was founded by Thomas Seath in 1845. Seath sold the business to Partickonian brothers Anthony and John Inglis in 1856 when he established the Rutherglen Shipyard. They added the slip dock in 1867, behind the three legged hoist in the foreground. It was from here that the PS *Waverley* was launched in October 1946. Harland & Wolff bought a controlling share of the company in 1919 adding it to their Clyde shipyards which included the Meadowside Yard on the other side of the Kelvin and the Govan Yard across the Clyde. The yard closed in October 1962 and lay abandoned for decades, becoming a surreal oasis of shrubland by the Clyde surrounded by warehouses and garages, it is now the site of the Riverside Museum.

Looking west from the Govan Ferry slip in 1986. The foreground of this photograph is now dominated by the new Govan Footbridge, the old ferry dock infilled to provide its approach. On the left bank of the Clyde is the former Fairfield Shipyard, at the time of the photograph Govan Shipbuilders. The ship under construction is the MS *Norsea*, built for North Sea Ferries and the largest passenger ship built on the Clyde since the *QE2*. On the right is the wharfage of the Meadowside Shipbuilding Yard, the travelling cranes of Meadowside Quay and towering above them the enormous Meadowside Granary built on another of Partick Thistle's former pitches. Building began in 1911 and the granary was extended in 1936, 1960 and 1967. High level gantries linked the four buildings, creating what was said to be the largest grain storage facility in the United Kingdom and the largest brick-built structure in Europe. The granary closed in 1988 and was demolished in 2002 to make way for riverside apartments. Though not without drama. An unexploded bomb was found during the demolition. In the distance stands the titan crane at the Barclay, Curle Shipyard in Whiteinch.